ERICA CASHAW

FINDING THE light WITHIN

AN INTERACTIVE GUIDE FOR SELF-AWARENESS AND GROWTH

Are you ready to return to yourself?

Finding the Light Within is a compassionate, interactive guide to personal growth, emotional healing, and radical self-awareness. Written by transformational coach Erica Cashaw, this book meets you where you are-with real-life reflections, affirmations, and assessments that help you name your feelings, challenge negative thoughts, and rediscover your purpose. Whether you're navigating life transitions, burnout, or simply craving deeper clarity, this guide invites you to slow down, tune in, and reclaim your light. With tools grounded in emotional intelligence, positive psychology, and lived experience, you'll build habits that support your mental wellness and inner peace. This isn't just a book-it's a journey home to yourself.

Finding the Light Within

By Erica Cashaw

US City of Publication

Paterson, New Jersey

ISBNs:
Paperback: 979-8-9923278-2-3
eBook: 979-8-9923278-3-0

LCCN: 2025908373

DEDICATION

To you—the reader—thank you for saying yes to this self-discovery journey. Your time is sacred, and I honor your decision to spend some of it with me.

Table of Contents

Foreword & Foundations

Finding the Light Within was developed from over a decade of hands-on experience in education, coaching, and personal growth. While I am not a licensed therapist, I've been trained in emotional intelligence, reflective practice, and social-emotional learning—through both formal education and real-world application. The tools you'll find here blend research-backed strategies with spirit-led insights. Each has been tested in classrooms, workshops, and one-on-one coaching sessions.

You may notice the influence of:
- Positive Psychology (Character Strengths, Growth Mindset)
- Social-Emotional Learning (SEL) Practices
- Reflective Journaling and Self-Inquiry
- Cognitive Behavioral Tools (Thought Reframing, Grounding)
- Life Coaching Methods (Self-Awareness, Personal Accountability)

To learn more or download printable versions of the worksheets and exercises,

visit www.EricaCashaw.com/resources.

Welcome + How to Use This Book

Welcome to Finding the Light Within. This guide was created for students, adults, professionals, and community leaders—anyone navigating life, seeking clarity, or ready to grow in purpose and peace.

Inside, you'll find a blend of self-reflection tools, practical assessments, and guided exercises to help you check in with yourself, uncover your strengths, and build habits that support your emotional and mental well-being.

I am not a licensed therapist, but I am a certified educator, a life coach, and a woman who has walked through both challenges and triumphs. This book was shaped by lived experiences, rooted in personal growth, and designed to support transformation—on your terms, in your time.

Use these pages however you need them. Move through them daily, weekly, or seasonally. You don't have to finish it all in one sitting. The goal is not speed—it's honesty, healing, and light.

Let's begin.

Section 1: Topics & Affirmations

In my everyday conversations—with family, friends, and especially through my work in alternative education and adult learning—I began to notice recurring emotional themes. These weren't just passing feelings; they were deep, often unspoken experiences many of us carry. That's why Finding the Light Within begins with real, raw topics.

These reflections are an invitation: a space to acknowledge your feelings, speak truth to them, and move toward greater clarity. It's important to pause, notice what you're thinking and feeling, give those emotions a name, and then begin to reframe them with truth. Because how can we discover the good, the light, and our purpose if we're buried under self-doubt, foggy thinking, and beliefs that were never really ours to begin with?

What is an affirmation?

An affirmation is a positive, intentional statement rooted in truth. It helps redirect your thoughts and center your energy on what's real and empowering. Words have the power to give life—or to dim your light.

Why are affirmations important?

Because our minds are always listening. The words we speak to ourselves shape how we see the world—and our place in it. Affirmations help us rewire limiting beliefs, soothe inner conflict, and reconnect with who we truly are.

Affirmation Practice Tips:

- Write them on sticky notes or mirrors
- Say them out loud during your morning routine
- Record your voice reading them—listen when you need grounding
- Journal how each one makes you feel over time

How to Use This Section:

Below, you'll find a selection of emotional themes—though I encourage you to add your own. Read the topic. Pause. Reflect. Sit with what comes up. Then read the affirmations slowly and intentionally. Let them land. When you're ready, respond to the reflective question at the end. Let this be a practice of returning to yourself.

Loneliness

What It Is:

Loneliness is more than being alone—it's the feeling of being disconnected, even when others are around. It may show up during transitions, losses, or when you feel unseen.

Affirmations:

- I am worthy of connection and support.
- This feeling is temporary; I can take steps to reconnect.
- I value my own company and know how to care for myself.
- I create space for meaningful connection.

Affirmation Practice:

Place your hand over your heart. Breathe deeply and remind yourself: connection begins within. You are already worthy of being seen and known.

Reflection Question:

Describe a time when you felt alone but continued moving forward. What helped?

Being Alone

What It Is:

Solitude is different from loneliness. Being alone can be a powerful time of reflection and growth—when it's intentional.

Affirmations:

- I am at peace in my own presence.

- Solitude gives me room to grow and reset.
- I use alone time to recharge, not retreat.
- I am learning to enjoy my own company.

Affirmation Practice:

Let silence be your companion for a moment. Sit with your thoughts and ask: What is solitude trying to teach me today?

Reflection Question:

How do you feel when you spend time alone? What benefits can solitude offer you?

Gloomy

What It Is:

We all have low-energy days or moments when the world feels heavy. That's okay. What matters is how you care for yourself during those times.

Affirmations:

- My feelings are valid, but they don't define me.
- I choose to move gently through this moment.
- I trust that brighter days are coming.
- I can name my emotions and still take action.

Affirmation Practice:

Light a candle, open a window, or simply pause. Repeat one affirmation softly—like you're offering kindness to a tired friend.

Reflection Question:

What helps you lift your mood or reset your focus on hard days?

Anger

What It Is:

Anger is a natural emotion. It often points to unmet needs, hurt, or boundaries being crossed. When expressed with care, anger can lead to clarity and change.

Affirmations:

- I am in control of how I respond to my emotions.
- I allow myself to feel anger without letting it take over.
- I release what no longer serves me.
- I can express my feelings in a healthy way.

Affirmation Practice:

Inhale for 4 counts. Exhale for 6. As you say the affirmations, let your voice carry strength and self-control. You can feel deeply and still respond with power.

Reflection Question:

What typically triggers your anger? How can you respond in a way that aligns with your values?

Happiness

What It Is:

Happiness isn't just a good day—it's often a habit built from small choices and moments of gratitude. It can coexist with challenges.

Affirmations:

- I choose to focus on what brings me joy.
- I create happiness through gratitude and perspective.
- I deserve to experience moments of peace and pleasure.
- Joy is not selfish—it's a form of strength.

Affirmation Practice:

Smile gently—even if it feels small. Choose one joy-filled phrase and let it echo in your mind like a song lyric that lifts you.

Reflection Question:

What activities, people, or moments bring you the most joy?

Negative Self-Talk

What It Is:

Negative self-talk shows up as inner criticism. It often repeats fears, doubts, or lies picked up from others. With awareness, you can challenge and reframe it.

Affirmations:

- I am enough as I am, while still growing.
- I choose words that build me up, not tear me down.
- I am learning to speak to myself with compassion.
- I can replace negative thoughts with truth.

Affirmation Practice:

Close your eyes and imagine speaking to your younger self. Which affirmation do they need to hear? Say it to them—and to yourself—with care.

Reflection Question:

What's one negative thought you hear often—and what's a truth you can say instead?

Stress

What It Is:

Stress is part of life, especially when we feel pulled in many directions. Recognizing it—and responding with care—is an essential part of managing it.

Affirmations:

- I am allowed to pause.

- I release what I can't control and focus on what I can.
- I have tools to create calm within myself.
- I'm doing the best I can—and that is enough today.

Affirmation Practice:

Release your shoulders. Drop your jaw. Breathe. Choose one affirmation to anchor you right now. Let it be your pause before the next step.

Reflection Question:

What are your current sources of stress? What's one small action you can take today to manage it?

Transition

What It Is:

Life is full of transitions—new schools, careers, relationships, or identities. Change can feel uncomfortable, but it's often a sign of growth.

Affirmations:

- I trust myself during seasons of change.
- Transition is not failure—it's forward movement.
- I am allowed to feel uncertain and still move forward.
- I carry lessons from my past into my future.

Affirmation Practice:

Think of a past change you survived. Hold that memory as you speak these affirmations, knowing you've done hard things before—and grown.

Reflection Question:

Think about a time when change pushed you to grow. What did you learn about yourself?

Purpose

What It Is:

Purpose is what gives life direction and meaning—your 'why.'

Affirmations:

- I am here for a reason.
- My purpose doesn't have to be perfect to be powerful.
- I trust that I'm being guided, even when the path isn't clear.
- I have the right to grow, evolve, and choose again.

Affirmation Practice:

Look at your hands. What are they capable of creating, holding, or doing? As you say the affirmations, imagine your purpose gently unfolding.

Reflection Question:

What makes you feel most alive or fulfilled? What's one step you can take toward that this week?

Confidence

What It Is:

Confidence is trust in your abilities, qualities, and judgment. It's not about perfection—it's about recognizing your worth and potential, even in uncertain moments.

Affirmations:

- I trust in my abilities and the knowledge I've gained.
- I am enough exactly as I am right now.
- I grow stronger with each challenge I face.
- My voice and perspective matter in every room.

Affirmation Practice:

Stand tall, feet grounded. Say one affirmation while looking at yourself in a mirror—or close your eyes and envision yourself succeeding.

Reflection Question:

When have you felt most confident? What internal or external factors contributed to that feeling?

Change & Uncertainty

What It Is:

Change is life's only constant. It brings both opportunity and discomfort. How we navigate uncertainty often defines our growth and resilience.

Affirmations:

- I embrace change as an opportunity for growth.
- I can adapt and thrive in new circumstances.
- Uncertainty doesn't mean unsafe—it means possibility.
- Each ending creates space for a new beginning.

Affirmation Practice:

Picture yourself walking a winding path. Each affirmation is a step forward. You don't need the full map—just trust the next step.

Reflection Question:

What has a past period of change or uncertainty taught you about yourself?

Self-Compassion

What It Is:

Self-compassion means treating yourself with the same kindness and understanding you would offer to a good friend during difficult times.

Affirmations:

- I deserve the same kindness I show to others.
- My mistakes and struggles are part of being human.
- I acknowledge my feelings without judgment.
- I forgive myself and choose to move forward with grace.

Affirmation Practice:

Hug yourself or wrap your arms across your chest. Say one affirmation as if offering grace to your best friend. You are just as deserving.

Reflection Question:

In what situations do you find it hardest to show yourself compassion—and how might you begin to change that pattern?

Resilience

What It Is:

Resilience is the capacity to recover from difficulties and adapt to change. It's not about avoiding hardship—it's about developing the strength to bounce back stronger.

Affirmations:

- I have overcome challenges before, and I can do it again.
- My strength grows with every obstacle I face.
- I bend without breaking when life gets hard.
- My history proves I am capable of surviving tough times.

Affirmation Practice:

List one challenge you've already overcome. As you say the affirmations, let that memory be proof of the strength still inside you.

Reflection Question:

What resources—internal or external—help you bounce back when life gets difficult?

Boundaries

What It Is:

Boundaries are the limits we set to protect our physical, emotional, and mental well-being. They define where we end and others begin, allowing for healthy relationships and self-respect.

Affirmations:

- I have the right to set limits that honor my needs.
- Saying "no" when necessary is an act of self-care.
- I communicate my boundaries with clarity and respect.
- My boundaries may change—and that's perfectly okay.

Affirmation Practice:

Say the affirmations as quiet declarations. Imagine a soft but steady "no" echoing in the background—not out of anger, but from self-respect.

Reflection Question:

In what area of your life do you need stronger boundaries right now? What's one small step you can take toward establishing them?

Section 2: Self-Discovery Assessments

Now that you've completed the Affirmations section, you're off to a powerful start. You've taken the first steps in grounding yourself with truth and intention.

This next section marks the second leg of our journey: Self-Discovery Assessments. Here, you'll begin to deepen your awareness, explore your inner world, and uncover the patterns, strengths, and opportunities that shape your experience.

Each assessment in this section is designed to help you explore a different part of who you are. You'll find a brief explanation of why the topic matters, followed by reflective statements and guiding questions.

How to Use This Section

- Read each set of statements carefully.
- Use the provided scale to rate how much each one resonates with you.
- Reflect after completing each assessment—what stands out? What surprised you?
- Be honest. This space is for you.
- Take your time. Let this be a quiet conversation between you and yourself—one that gently leads you back to your truth.

Personal Strengths Assessment

Why It Matters:

Knowing your strengths builds confidence and direction. When you understand what you do well, you can make more aligned decisions, strengthen relationships, and approach goals with clarity.

Instructions:

Rate how much you agree with each statement using the scale below:
1 = Strongly Disagree | 2 = Disagree | 3 = Neutral | 4 = Agree | 5 = Strongly Agree

Statements:

- I'm good at coming up with new ideas.
- I enjoy helping others solve their problems.
- I'm skilled at organizing and planning.
- I'm comfortable speaking in front of groups.
- I'm patient and good at teaching others.
- I'm analytical and enjoy working with data.
- I'm creative and express myself through art or writing.
- I'm good at motivating and inspiring others.
- I'm detail-oriented and thorough in my work.
- I'm adaptable and thrive in changing environments.

Reflection Questions:

- How do your top strengths align with the roles you play in life?
- What strengths do others often notice in you?
- Is there a strength you want to develop more—and why?

Learning Style Assessment

Why It Matters:

Understanding how you learn best can help you approach school, work, or personal growth with more ease and confidence. It allows you to tailor your environment and strategies for better focus and retention.

Instructions:

Rate each statement using the following scale:
1 = Strongly Disagree | 2 = Disagree | 3 = Neutral | 4 = Agree | 5 = Strongly Agree

Visual Learning Statements:

- I remember information better when I see it written down.
- I prefer instructions that include diagrams, charts, or pictures.
- I often visualize concepts in my mind to understand them.
- I take detailed notes during lessons or meetings.
- I find color-coding information helpful for organizing my thoughts.

Auditory Learning Statements:

- I learn best by listening to explanations or discussions.
- I remember conversations in detail.
- I prefer verbal instructions over written ones.
- I often read aloud when trying to understand complex material.
- I find that background music helps me focus rather than distracts me.

Kinesthetic Learning Statements:

- I understand concepts better when I can physically handle objects.
- I tend to use hand gestures when speaking.
- I prefer to learn by doing rather than by reading or listening.
- I have difficulty sitting still for long periods.
- I remember information better when I associate it with movement or action.

Scoring:

- Add your totals for statements 1–5: _____ (Visual preference)
- Add your totals for statements 6–10: _____ (Auditory preference)
- Add your totals for statements 11–15: _____ (Kinesthetic preference)

Your highest score indicates your primary learning style—though most people use a combination.

Reflection Questions:

- How can you adapt your learning environment to support your preferred style?
- When has your learning style helped—or hindered—you?
- What strategies from your non-dominant styles might help you grow?

Coping Under Pressure Evaluation

Why It Matters:

How you respond to pressure impacts your focus, relationships, and ability to follow through. Awareness of your patterns helps you create more grounded responses.

Instructions:

For each scenario, choose the option that best reflects your usual response.

Scenarios:

When facing a tight deadline:

a) I make a plan and stick to it.
b) I delay but get it done.
c) I freeze or avoid it.
When someone criticizes me:
a) I reflect on it and grow.
b) I feel hurt, but try to learn.
c) I take it personally and shut down.

When plans change suddenly:

a) I adapt quickly.
b) I stress but keep moving.
c) I feel stuck.

When I have too many tasks:

a) I prioritize and delegate.
b) I push through under pressure.
c) I procrastinate or give up.

When emotions run high:

a) I breathe and stay grounded.
b) I get reactive but catch myself.
c) I lash out or shut down.

When deadlines stack up:

a) I stay focused and create a plan.
b) I rush and feel scattered.
c) I shut down or withdraw.

When I'm in a group under pressure:

a) I stay composed and encourage others.
b) I participate but feel anxious.
c) I go quiet or disengage.

When disappointment happens:

a) I acknowledge it and move forward.
b) I dwell but bounce back.
c) I carry it with me.

When a task is unclear:

a) I ask for clarity or break it down.
b) I guess and hope for the best.
c) I avoid it.

When I'm overwhelmed:

a) I ask for help or slow down.
b) I try to handle it alone.
c) I escape into distractions or avoid it.

Scoring:

- Mostly A's: Strong coping skills
- Mostly B's: You're managing, but may benefit from stronger habits
- Mostly C's: Your stress patterns may need support and new strategies

Reflection Questions:

- What types of pressure affect you most?
- Which habits help you stay steady under stress?

Emotional Intelligence Quick Check

Why It Matters:

This quick check provides a snapshot of how you relate to your own emotions—and the emotions of others.

Instructions:

Rate each statement from 1 (Rarely) to 5 (Always).

Statements:

- I can name my emotions in real time.
- I stay calm in emotionally charged moments.
- I notice how others are feeling without them saying it.
- I think before I respond.
- I bounce back after emotional setbacks.

Scoring:

- 20–25: High emotional intelligence
- 15–19: Developing emotional skills
- Below 15: Growth opportunity in self-awareness and regulation

Reflection Questions:

- Which response was most difficult to rate?
- How do your emotional skills affect your daily interactions?

Emotional Intelligence Full Assessment

Why It Matters:

This full check-in explores key components of emotional intelligence, including self-awareness, self-regulation, social awareness, and relationship skills.

Instructions:

Rate each statement from 1 (Never) to 5 (Always).

Self-Awareness:

- I notice my emotions as they rise.
- I know how my emotions influence my behavior.
- I recognize my strengths and areas to grow.
- I reflect on my emotions regularly.
- I notice when my mood shifts.

Self-Management:

- I manage stress effectively.
- I pause before reacting in tough situations.
- I follow through on commitments.
- I adapt to changes easily.
- I stay motivated through challenges.

Social Awareness:

- I read the room well in group settings.
- I notice non-verbal cues.
- I value other people's perspectives.
- I offer support when someone is struggling.
- I listen to understand, not just respond.

Relationship Skills:

- I resolve conflict in healthy ways.
- I encourage and motivate others.
- I give clear and respectful feedback.

- I build strong relationships over time.
- I show up with empathy and consistency.

Scoring:

- 80–100: High emotional intelligence
- 60–79: Functional, with areas for growth
- 40–59: Opportunity to strengthen core skills

Reflection Questions:

- Which domain do you feel strongest in?
- Which behaviors do you want to improve?

Listening Skills Evaluation

Why It Matters:

Listening well builds trust, improves relationships, and fosters deeper understanding.

Instructions:

Rate each statement from 1 (Never) to 5 (Always).

Statements:

- I focus fully when someone is speaking.
- I avoid interrupting.
- I ask follow-up questions.
- I reflect back what I hear.
- I stay patient when others take time to express themselves.
- I listen without jumping to solutions.
- I give non-verbal feedback (nodding, eye contact).
- I'm aware when I stop listening and redirect my focus.
- I recognize emotion in the speaker's tone.
- I hold space for others without judgment.

Scoring:

- 40–50: Strong listener
- 30–39: Good foundation
- Below 30: Listening skills need more attention

Reflection Questions:

- What distracts you from listening well?
- What helps you stay present in conversations?

Creativity Assessment

Why It Matters:

Creativity fuels problem-solving, innovation, and emotional expression. It's not just about art—it's about how you think, imagine, and adapt.

Instructions:

Rate each statement from 1 (Strongly Disagree) to 5 (Strongly Agree).

Statements:

- I enjoy exploring new ideas or approaches.
- I come up with original solutions to problems.
- I feel energized when creating something new.
- I'm open to experimenting and learning from mistakes.
- I enjoy brainstorming or imagining possibilities.
- I like to connect seemingly unrelated ideas.
- I use writing, drawing, or design to express myself.
- I ask "what if" questions often.
- I take creative risks, even when unsure.
- I make space for creativity in my daily life.

Scoring:

- 45–50: Highly creative
- 30–44: Growing creatively
- Below 30: Opportunity to reengage your creativity

Reflection Questions:

- Where do you express your creativity most?
- What's one creative activity you'd like to try again or explore?

Procrastination Tendency Quiz

Why It Matters:

Understanding why you delay tasks can help you build stronger focus, follow-through, and time management strategies.

Instructions:

Rate each statement from 1 (Never) to 5 (Always).

Statements:

- I avoid starting tasks, even when important.
- I feel overwhelmed looking at big projects.
- I say "I'll do it later," but forget.
- I wait for motivation before acting.
- I get easily distracted once I start.
- I tend to rush at the last minute.
- I often miss deadlines or cut it close.
- I work better under pressure (but it's stressful).
- I avoid tasks that feel hard or unclear.
- I feel anxious when I think about unfinished work.

Scoring:

- 45–50: High procrastination tendencies
- 30–44: Occasional delay habits
- Below 30: Strong follow-through skills

Reflection Questions:

- What triggers your delay?
- What helps you take the first step?

Physical Self-Discovery Check-In

Why It Matters:

Your physical well-being impacts your focus, energy, and emotional regulation. Listening to your body helps you stay grounded and resilient.

Instructions:

Rate each statement from 1 (Strongly Disagree) to 5 (Strongly Agree).

Statements:

- I wake up feeling rested.
- I stay hydrated throughout the day.
- I move my body regularly.
- I eat meals that nourish me.
- I notice when I need rest and respond.
- I take breaks during long work or study periods.
- I feel strong and energized in my body.
- I go for medical care when needed.
- I understand how emotions affect my body.
- I feel in tune with my physical needs.

Reflection Questions:

- What's one thing your body is asking for right now?
- How do you take care of yourself during busy seasons?

Relationship Assessment (Romantic & Platonic)

Why It Matters:

Healthy relationships build our confidence, resilience, and sense of belonging. They support emotional safety and personal growth.

Instructions:

Rate each statement from 1 (Strongly Disagree) to 5 (Strongly Agree).

Statements:

- I feel emotionally safe in this relationship.
- We communicate honestly and clearly.
- We resolve conflict respectfully.
- There's mutual support and understanding.
- We respect each other's boundaries.
- I can express my needs and be heard.
- We both contribute to the relationship.
- We celebrate each other's wins.
- I feel valued and seen as I am.
- We grow together—not apart.

Scoring:

- 45–50: Strong, healthy relationship
- 30–44: Some areas may need attention
- Below 30: May require deeper reflection or support

Reflection Questions:

- Which relationship in your life feels healthiest?
- What's one change that could strengthen connection?

Life Alignment Chart

Why It Matters:

Balance across different life areas helps you manage stress, maintain energy, and avoid burnout. Checking in allows you to adjust before things feel overwhelming.

Instructions:

Rate your current level of satisfaction in each category from 1 (Very Dissatisfied) to 10 (Very Satisfied).

1.Family Time, communication, boundaries, connection, support
2. Friends Authenticity, availability, mutual joy, growth
3. Associates Networking, mentorship, professional allies
4. Physical Well-Being Movement, nutrition, sleep, energy levels
5. Mental Wellness Clarity, mindset, boundaries, stimulation
6. Emotional Wellness Self-regulation, emotional expression, healing tools
7. Spiritual Alignment Faith practices, connection to God, purpose-driven living
8. Love Receiving and giving love, feeling secure, valued
9. Intimacy Emotional, physical, and spiritual closeness (including with self and partner)
10. Career / Business Fulfillment, growth, alignment, financial flow
11. Environment Home, workspace, digital space, and energy hygiene
12. Fun / Play Joy, adventure, laughter, lightheartedness
13. Lifestyle Daily rhythm, habits, time use, simplicity or abundance
14. Creativity Art, expression, innovation, sacred making
15. Purpose Legacy, calling, impact, alignment with soul work
16. Finances Stability, goals, giving, saving, earning, peace

16 Dimension Life Alignment Chart

Rate each area from 1 (very dissatisfied) to 10 (fully aligned/satisfied). Use the spaces below to reflect on what's working well and what needs your attention.

Category	Rating (1–10)	What's Working Well?	Needs Attention?
Family			
Friends			
Associates			
Physical Well-Being			
Mental Wellness			
Emotional Wellness			
Spiritual Alignment			
Love			
Intimacy			
Career / Business			
Environment			
Fun / Play			
Lifestyle			
Creativity			
Purpose			
Finances			

Scoring:

There's no single total score—just patterns. Use your results to identify where attention or support is most needed.

Reflection Questions:

- Which area is currently your strongest? Which is lowest?
- What part of your life needs more support right now?
- What's one small step you can take toward better balance?

Career Values and Interests Assessment

Why It Matters:

Knowing your interests and values helps you align your work with what truly matters to you, leading to greater satisfaction and clarity in your professional path.

Instructions:

Rate how interested you would be in each activity, using this scale:
1 = Not at all interested | 5 = Very interested

Building and Creating:

- Working with my hands to build or fix things
- Designing products, spaces, or systems
- Creating physical objects from raw materials
- Operating machinery or equipment
- Working on projects with tangible results

Helping and Supporting:

- Teaching or mentoring others
- Providing care or assistance to people in need
- Helping people solve personal problems
- Working for causes that benefit communities
- Supporting others' personal or professional growth

Analyzing and Investigating:

- Researching complex questions or problems
- Working with data and statistics
- Conducting experiments or tests
- Analyzing information to draw conclusions
- Investigating how things work

Organizing and Managing:

- Creating efficient systems or procedures
- Managing projects or coordinating activities
- Keeping detailed records or files
- Following step-by-step processes
- Organizing events or workflows

Influencing and Leading:

- Persuading others to adopt ideas or take action
- Leading teams or directing activities
- Starting or running a business
- Negotiating agreements or resolving conflicts
- Public speaking or performing

Creative Expression:

- Writing stories, articles, or content
- Creating visual art or designs
- Performing music, dance, or drama
- Developing creative concepts or campaigns
- Finding innovative solutions to problems

Scoring:

Add your scores for each group. Your highest categories reveal the areas where your natural interests and potential career paths align.

Reflection Questions:

- What patterns do you notice in your top-scoring categories?
- How do these interests align with your current work or studies?
- What specific careers combine your top interests?
- If you started a business, what products or services would reflect your strengths?

Communication Style Assessment

Why It Matters:

Understanding your communication style can help you connect more clearly with others, avoid conflict, and share your ideas more effectively.

Instructions:

Rate each statement from 1 (Not at all like me) to 5 (Very much like me).

Statements:

- I tend to speak directly and get straight to the point.
- I prefer providing all the details when explaining something.
- I consider how others might feel before speaking.
- I enjoy debating ideas and challenging assumptions.
- I use stories and examples to make my points.
- I choose my words carefully before speaking.
- I'm comfortable expressing disagreement.
- I ask questions to understand others' perspectives.
- I use humor or lightheartedness in my communication.
- I prefer writing my thoughts rather than speaking them.
- I'm aware of my body language when communicating.
- I find it easy to speak up in group settings.
- I notice subtle cues in how others respond to me.

Scoring Insights:

- High on 1, 4, 7, 12: Direct/Assertive
- High on 2, 5, 9, 13: Expressive/Narrative
- High on 3, 8, 11, 13, 15: Empathetic/Receptive
- High on 6, 10, 14: Analytical/Thoughtful

Reflection Questions:

- How does your communication style shift in different settings?
- When has your style helped you—and when has it caused tension?
- Which communication styles do you find most challenging to connect with?

Decision-Making Style Inventory

Why It Matters:

The way you make decisions affects every part of your life. Becoming aware of your natural style helps you make more confident and balanced choices.

Instructions:

Rate each statement from 1 (Strongly Disagree) to 5 (Strongly Agree).

Statements:

- I gather as much information as possible before deciding.
- I trust my gut feeling when making choices.
- I consider how my decisions will affect others.
- I weigh the pros and cons carefully.
- I make decisions quickly and efficiently.
- I consider my personal values when making choices.
- I prefer to sleep on important decisions.
- I ask for advice from people I trust.
- I think about the long-term implications of my choices.
- I'm comfortable making unpopular decisions if necessary.
- I reflect on past experiences when making new decisions.
- I consider worst-case scenarios before deciding.

Scoring:

- Analytical Thinking (1, 4, 9, 12): _____
- Intuitive Thinking (2, 5, 7, 11): _____
- Values-Based Thinking (3, 6, 8, 10): _____

Your highest score indicates your dominant decision-making style, though most people use a mix depending on the situation.

Reflection Questions:

- How does your style serve you—and where might it limit you?
- Which decisions have felt most aligned with your strengths?
- How might incorporating less-used styles help you make more holistic choices?

Section 3: Real-Life Transformations

Why It Matters:

Theory becomes powerful when we see it in action. In this section, you'll meet real people (names and details changed) who used the tools and assessments in this book to navigate real challenges.

These case studies are bridges—connecting your self-discovery work to real-world application. As you read, you may recognize pieces of your own journey or uncover new possibilities for growth.

Each person began with curiosity, some uncertainty, and a willingness to reflect. Their stories show that transformation isn't just about insight—it's about action.

How to Use This Section:

- Notice which stories resonate most—they may reflect parts of your own life
- Pay attention to which tools helped each person most
- Consider how similar approaches could support your journey
- Remember: growth looks different for everyone—there's no "right way" to evolve

Case Study 1: From Disengaged to Directed

Situation:

Maurice, 18, was a high school senior who was frequently late or absent. He felt traditional education didn't connect with his future goals. Though passionate about two career paths, he couldn't see the point in finishing school.

Challenge:

Maurice struggled with motivation and time management. He lacked understanding of what it would truly take—financially and academically—to pursue either career. He also underestimated the value of completing high school.

Tools Used:

- Career Values and Interests Assessment
- SMART Goal Setting
- Personal Strengths Assessment
- Decision-Making Style Inventory
- Purpose & Confidence Affirmations

Outcome:

Through coaching, Maurice explored the actual steps required for his career goals, including salary research, cost of living, and minimum education levels. He created a Plan A and Plan B, identified strengths and gaps, and mapped SMART goals to finish high school on time. He later enrolled in a vocational program aligned with his passion and recently graduated, ready for the next chapter.

Coach's Corner:

What stood out most was how quickly transformation started once Maurice felt seen. His frustration wasn't laziness—it was misalignment. When we linked his vision with real steps, his drive became unstoppable.

Case Study 2: The Returner's Journey

Situation:

Denise, a nighttime adult learner balancing work and motherhood, showed up to class—but barely. She doubted whether college could fit into her already overloaded life.

Challenge:

Denise was caught between survival and growth. Low energy, time pressure, and a fragile sense of confidence kept her stuck. She couldn't see how long-term goals could coexist with short-term demands.

Tools Used:

- Time Management Tools & Life Alignment Chart
- SMART Goal Setting
- Confidence & Self-Compassion Affirmations
- Decision-Making Style Inventory
- Support Systems Mapping

Outcome:

Denise developed a realistic timeline that accounted for work, childcare, and rest. She delayed college by a year, but she never quit. With grace and structure, she earned her associate degree—and now sees herself as capable and deserving of more.

Coach's Corner:

Denise didn't need a miracle—she needed a plan that honored her reality. Once she viewed her path as flexible, not fixed, she unlocked her own permission to grow.

Case Study 3:
Rediscovering Self Beyond the Roles

Situation:

Lareese, a longtime caregiver and professional, was nearing a new life season with no roadmap. With her children grown, she was asking herself, 'Now what?'

Challenge:

Lareese's self-worth was tied to productivity. Slowing down felt wrong, even though she was tired. Her busyness had become armor hiding old grief and identity questions.

Tools Used:

- Life Alignment Chart
- Self-Care Pattern Assessment
- Purpose & Self-Compassion Affirmations
- Key Reflection Questions
- Creativity & Career Interests Assessments
- Therapy Referral

Outcome:

Lareese began healing. She reconnected with hobbies, released guilt, and embraced rest. She's now journaling, dreaming about consulting, and shifting from 'What do I do?' to 'Who am I becoming?'

Coach's Corner:

Lareese's breakthrough came when she realized rest wasn't laziness—it was restoration. Letting go of old narratives allowed space for joy to return.

Case Study 4:
From Employee to Entrepreneur

Situation:

Marquis, a husband and father, was burned out from his 9–5 and longed to build something of his own—but feared risking his family's stability.

Challenge:

This wasn't just a career pivot—it was a personal one. Marquise had to reimagine his identity and build clarity and confidence while honoring his home life and financial responsibilities.

Tools Used:

- SMART Goals & Timeline Mapping
- Life Alignment
- Decision-Making Style Inventory
- Self-Care Pattern Assessment
- Purpose & Confidence Affirmations
- Communication & Partnership Strategy

Outcome:

With his family's rhythm in mind, Marquis mapped out a strategic transition. He discussed expectations and boundaries with his wife, created financial checkpoints, and now moves forward steadily—building a business and a life that reflects his purpose.

Coach's Corner:

Marquis reminded me that purpose doesn't always demand a leap—it calls for alignment. When strategy, timing, and communication line up, bold steps start to feel doable.

Section 4: Worksheets for Growth & Grounding

You're deep into this journey now—pause and take that in. You've already done powerful work, and now you're entering the final stretch.

This section provides grounding worksheets to help you process, integrate, and act on everything you've explored. These tools are designed to bring clarity and connection when life feels messy or uncertain.

How to Use This Section:

- Reflect on recent emotions or challenges
- Re-center yourself during stress or decision-making
- Clarify your goals and next steps
- Stay grounded in your values and vision

Whether you're journaling, planning, or just breathing deeply—let these pages meet you where you are.

Thought Observation Worksheet

Purpose:

To help you notice your thoughts without judgment. This builds emotional awareness and gives you space to decide which thoughts to keep—and which to gently release.

Instructions:

Set a timer for 5–10 minutes. Find a quiet space. As thoughts arise, write them down. Don't try to change or censor them—just observe.

Thought Cloud Reflections:

(Use this space to jot freely.)

Reflection Questions:

- Were your thoughts mostly calm, anxious, critical, hopeful, or something else?
- Did any themes repeat?
- What thoughts do you want to explore further—or let go of?

Five Senses Grounding Exercise

Purpose:

To reduce anxiety and bring your awareness back to the present moment through sensory connection.

Instructions:

Find a quiet spot. Use your senses to slowly respond to the prompts below.

Grounding Prompts:

- 5 things I can see: ________________________________
- 4 things I can feel (touch): __________________________
- 3 things I can hear: ________________________________
- 2 things I can smell: ______________________________
- 1 thing I can taste: ______________________________

Reflection Questions:

- How did your body feel before and after the exercise?
- What part helped you feel most grounded?

Body Scan Meditation Worksheet

Purpose:

To increase body awareness and help identify where you're holding tension or emotion physically.

Instructions:

Sit or lie down in a calm space. Close your eyes if comfortable. Slowly bring attention to each part of your body, from head to feet. Note sensations or tension you observe.

Body Awareness Notes:

- Head: ______________________________
- Face/Jaw: ___________________________
- Neck/Shoulders: _____________________
- Arms/Hands: ________________________
- Chest: ______________________________
- Abdomen: ___________________________
- Back: _______________________________
- Hips: _______________________________
- Legs/Feet: ___________________________

Reflection Questions:

- Where did you notice the most tension—or comfort?
- What surprised you about how your body feels?
- How might you respond differently to your body's needs this week?

Section 5: Wrap Up My Self-Discovery Snapshot

Take a moment to capture the insights, strengths, and truths you uncovered during this journey. This is your personal snapshot—a reminder of how far you've come and a compass for the road ahead.

Personal Strengths • Top 3 Strengths I Identified:

Learning Style:

Primary Learning Style:

Other Insights About How I Learn Best:

Coping Under Pressure

My Coping Style Summary:

One Strategy That Helps Me Stay Grounded:

Emotional Intelligence

Quick Check Score Range: [ ] High (20–25) [ ] Growing (15–19) [ ] Opportunity for Growth (below 15)

One Skill I Want to Strengthen:

Listening Skills

Listening Score:

My Strengths as a Listener:

Creativity

Creativity Score:

How I Express My Creativity Most:

Procrastination Patterns

Procrastination Score:

Biggest Trigger for Delay:

New Focus Strategy I Want to Try:

Physical Self-Discovery

One Key Insight About My Body's Needs:

Relationships

Relationship Health Score (Romantic/Platonic):

One Relationship I Want to Nurture or Protect:

Life Alignment Chart

Strongest Area:

Area Needing the Most Attention:

Career Values & Interests

Top Career Interests Identified:

Communication Style

Primary Communication Style(s):

What Helps Me Connect Better:

Decision-Making Style

Primary Style: [ ] Analytical [ ] Intuitive [ ] Values-Based [ ] Blended

One Way I Want to Strengthen My Decision-Making:

Final Reflection

The Three Biggest Things I Learned About Myself Are:

Closing Note

This snapshot is a mirror of your resilience, clarity, and courage.

Keep it close.

Update it as you grow.

Let it remind you: You are capable. You are evolving. You are already light.

Key Reflection Questions

Purpose:

To support deeper self-discovery, clarify your values, and inspire intentional growth.

Prompts:

- What are three words that best describe you right now?
- What activities make you lose track of time?
- What are your top three values in life?
- What does success mean to you today?
- What's one skill or habit you want to improve?
- What helps you stay grounded during emotional challenges?
- Who are the most important people in your life—and why?
- What's a belief or behavior you're ready to change?
- What would your younger self be proud of today?
- What would your future self thank you for starting now?

Closing Reflections

If you've made it to this page, pause and breathe. Honor that.
You've shown up for yourself. You've leaned into self-discovery and created space for growth. Whether you journaled deeply, paused between pages, or simply planted seeds for future reflection—know this: the light within you is real. You've taken steps to protect it, nurture it, and let it shine.

Life will keep shifting. Some days will bring clarity, others confusion. But now, you have language, insight, and tools to guide you.
Keep coming back to these pages. Keep asking questions. Keep showing up.
And above all—keep choosing yourself.

Call to Action

You've done the inner work. Now what?

- Share what you've learned. Start a conversation.
- Start something new. Whether it's a journaling habit, a next goal, or simply pausing more often —take one step forward.
- Stay connected. Join the coaching community, bring this work to your school or organization, or explore more resources at EricaCashaw.com.

Your light matters. And the world needs what's inside you.

With love,
Erica (Coach E) Cashaw

About the Author

Erica Cashaw—also known as Coach E—is a transformational coach, educator, and inspirational author committed to helping people navigate life with purpose and power.

Through her writing, coaching, and speaking, Erica empowers individuals from all walks of life—students, adults, professionals, and community leaders—to reflect, grow, and rediscover the light within.

Her work blends years of experience in education, personal development, and community engagement. Whether she's guiding adult learners, coaching clients, or leading workshops, Erica brings a message of resilience, clarity, and self-worth to every space she enters.

Finding the Light Within is a heartfelt guide for anyone in transition—whether returning to school, starting fresh, building a new chapter, or simply reconnecting with themselves. It's a powerful companion for classrooms, conferences, coaching circles, and quiet personal moments.

Erica is the founder of Elizabeth Patrice Coaching and Consulting, LLC, and the visionary behind EricaCashaw.com, where her mission continues—one book, one session, one breakthrough at a time.

Discover More by Erica Cashaw

Currently Available:

- Conversations with My Father: Heartfelt prayers and reflections
- My Grief Journal: A guided support tool for navigating loss
- Conversations with My Father Reaction Workbook: Companion workbook

Coming Soon:

- Maintaining Light Within: A self-care guide to sustaining personal peace
- Love, Peace, and Happiness: Reflections on life's core values
- Starting Your Conversations: 31-Day Prayer Challenge & Workbook
- Conversations with My Father: Volumes 2 and 3

For Learners & Leaders:

- Alternative Educator Guidebooks
- GED to PhD: Growth strategies for every stage
- Coaching Workbooks: Personal development for all ages

Explore more at EricaCashaw.com

DISCLAIMER

This book is intended for personal growth and reflection. It is not a substitute for licensed mental health care. While Erica Cashaw is a certified educator and life coach, she is not a licensed therapist.
Any tools or frameworks referenced (e.g., Emotional Intelligence, VIA Strengths, CBT-based techniques) are shared through the author's original lens and are meant for educational and self-development use only.

Made in United States
Orlando, FL
05 October 2025

70464270R00033